Pepper Learns Her Colors

PAGE PUBLISHING
Conneaut Lake, PA

First originally published by Page Publishing 2024

ISBN 979-8-89315-493-1 (pbk)
ISBN 979-8-89315-502-0 (digital)

Printed in the United States of America

Pepper Learns Her Colors

MARIAH BARGA

Pepper's owners are at work. She is excited to wait for them to come home.

She is ready to explore her colors while her owners are gone.

Pepper has a red collar that has her name on it.

Pepper likes to sit on her brown couch to look outside of her sun room.

Pepper loves to play with her blue duck, which is her favorite toy.

When Pepper is hungry, she eats her lunch out of her yellow food bowl.

After eating, Pepper is tired. She is ready to take a nap on her purple pillow.

When Pepper wakes up from her nap, she is ready to play fetch with her orange ball.

Pepper is happy when she sees her owners driving down the road in their green car.

Pepper is excited to tell her owners all the colors that she learned today!

About the Author

Mariah Barga is from the small town of North Star, Ohio. She has always loved reading from a young age and always wanted to share her passion for reading with others.

Pepper is a close family member's dog and was the inspiration behind this story.

Printed in the USA
CPSIA information can be obtained
at www.ICGtesting.com
CBHW062017210924
14613CB00066B/1237

9 798893 154931